C000103007

VICE

DOs & DON'Ts

400 NEW JOKES FROM THE FUNNIEST MAGAZINE COLUMN TO EVER EXIST IN THE HISTORY OF THE UNIVERSE

CANONGATE

Edinburgh · London · New York · Melbourne

Also Available:

THE WORLD
ACCORDING TO VICE

EDITED BY
Andy Capper
Bruno Bayley
Piers Martin
Imogen Bellotti

EDITOR IN CHIEF VICE GLOBAL
Andy Capper

DESIGNER
Imogen Bellotti

WORDS
Vice Staff

VICE FOUNDERS
Suroosh Alvi
Shane Smith

VICE MEDIA GROUP EU CEO
Andrew Creighton

THANKS TO
Dan Franklin
Jon Elek
Jenny Lord
The Fat Jew
Johnny Ryan
Nate Igor Smith
Nicholas Gazin
Mike de Leon
Maggie Lee
Vito Fun
Brenda Staudenmaier

First published in Great Britain in 2011 by Canongate Books
14 High Street, Edinburgh EH1 1TE

1

Excerpts from the original "*Vice* Guide to Everything"
originally published in v2n8, "The DOs and DON'Ts Issue".

British Library Cataloguing-in-Publication Data
A catalogue record for this book is available on request from
the British Library

ISBN 978 1 84767 970 3

Printed and bound in Spain by mccgraphics

www.vice.com

www.canongate.tv

INTRODUCTION

The first thing most people do when they pick up a copy of Vice *is turn to the DOs & DON'Ts. Introduced into the magazine more than a decade ago as a way of fitting fashion into our pages, they've become a mainstay of* Vice, *and one of our most popular reads.*

By way of an introduction to this volume of the last five years of DOs & DON'Ts, two of Vice*'s editors, Andy Capper and Thomas Morton, who between them have written many of the captions, discuss the enduring popularity of making fun of people's clothes.*

VICE Employee 1: How would you describe the DOs & DON'Ts to somebody who'd never heard of them?

VICE Employee 2: Pictures of people with funny captions about their pants, though I guess in the UK I'd have to say trousers.

VE 1: Yeah, our reporters risk their lives venturing into some of the most dangerous places in the world, but all anyone cares about is when we make a joke about some unsuspecting person's tits.

VE 2:: It's true, an insanely large number of people look at the DOs & DON'Ts. And there are definitely people out there who only know *Vice* through the DOs & DON'Ts and couldn't give a shit about what music we like or how Marina Abramovic prepared for her latest show.

They are immensely popular in spite of the standard charge of "not being as good as they used to be", and mostly because pictures + caption is super-amenable to quick, cheap comedy. Plus it's so easy to spend three hours just clicking through months of them online. At the same time, we try to put a little more effort into them than, "Check out this twat in the sweater. What a loser, right?"

VE 1: I always find I write the funnier ones when I'm really hungover.

VE 2: I haven't figured out when my funniest ones are. The ones I think are hilarious usually get pilloried in the comments. Then there are cast-offs that I put up for the weekend where people go ape-shit over a turn of phrase, or the fact that I called the person Carl. It's a mystery.

Having a tall friend is great in a fight, because he can come in and absorb all the punches. But having a tall friend who's also willing to absorb all the fag-bashing that leads to the punches is about as close as it gets to having your own personal stunt double.

G-Unit may have fallen off in record sales but at least they're still out there hustling for that paper.

Isn't he supposed to have open sores on his face and a mongrel dog that's dying of starvation whimpering into a half empty bowl of cider? He's like if Urban Outfitters did a line called "Distressed Rancid".

Since the bogeyman retired, big sisters have been scaring their siblings with stories of the Sex Squad Man who is under your bed right now and can't wait to tickle you.

DOs

Oh, to be wheeled to the banks of the river Styx by an immaculately attired angel of death who smells like lilies and brimstone and softly murmurs songs of praise in a stately baritone.

We generally don't like twinks but this is kind of OK. Anyone who can mix Andrew Cunanan with *My Own Private Idaho* is at least worthy of a little...

What the fuck do these disgusting pieces of sugar-filled white garbage need Bluetooths for? So the TV can call them? "HEY MOM—WE R STILL IN PARKING LOT—MARKS YAWNING—CAN WE GO—NEED TO GET BACK TO CONT. SHITTY LIVES."

Losing your leg at a Prodigy concert must be fucking harsh.

Your testicles have to get some fresh air once in a while. In fact, letting them run around the block in the snow is actually beneficial for sperm production. Don't forget to put a pair of sunglasses on them though. Balls have very sensitive eyes.

Yeah, cram it in your maw with those trembling fucking fingers. Show her who's the boss around here. Show that chicken and mushroom tartlet how you're sick of taking the train to work at 8 AM every day for 25 grand a year just to wait on tourists browsing expensive shoes.

If rappers started dressing like this fruitcake maybe I'd like their music again.

"Yessss! I'm totally being fucked by a famous guy! Hope nobody can see us."

Teaching your kid to fly is pretty impressive, we'll admit, but it still doesn't make up for all the racist shit.

What'll you give me if I suck all the old lentil soup, pot seeds and mental illness out of his beard?

"Oh, you haven't met Gerry's new girlfriend Marie yet? Classy broad. I think she's going to be out tonight."

SHOTS If someone buys you a shot, you have to do it, no matter what. If you're too hungover or the bar is about to close, you can pretend to do it by throwing it over your shoulder, but if you get caught that person has the right to never speak to you again. It is also considered good form to match your friend shot-for-shot. This is a matter of not asking your buddy to do something you wouldn't do yourself.

DOs

Fuck being thin and good looking. Most girls just want to hang around with plump bearded guys who are hilarious at parties and always have coke. If this guy was famous he'd probably be able to fuck them as well.

I don't know if it's male or female and frankly I don't care. I just want to rub my asshole up and down its face until it starts yodelling for mercy.

Look at how smug this fucking genius is about the worst mistake of his life so far. Just how much TV did his dad not let him watch?

DOs

If you live in a first-world country and you don't play video games while shitting (eating on the toilet works too), then I don't think you get what we're trying to do here.

You don't have to be gay to feel the urge to let this glitter-bear ejaculate on you. I don't even think you need to be horny.

You can say what you want about the meatheads who go around stealing bicylcles, but they've got the "sporty prison rape" look down to a T.

Here's to the black hoodie. Even tie-dyed space clowns from a freezing planet with an unbreathable atmosphere composed mainly of LSD can use it to pull their outfit together and make their style appear totally effortless.

DOs

When you hit 30 you can either go the way of the rural indie artist guy or you can shave your head, switch t-shirts to polos, and be the old city hardcore guy.

It's one thing to be the coked-up party animal who puts on a gold dress and lets his uncircumcised dick flop around just to be hilarious, but then to also start releasing awful farts that burn the nostrils? That's gangster.

After putting us through nearly two decades of maternity wear, black teens have basically earned a free pass on whatever look they want. Even chiptune nerd.

Yes, this is funny. Don't be a nerd.

Jesus Christ, what a fucking grill! That face looks like it's absorbed every problem every person in the whole world has ever had, and that includes diarrhoea.

In Milan, the hot new style for men this season is to look like a male prostitute in his boxer shorts calmly leaving the scene after brutally murdering an enema-obsessed priest who took it too far this time.

"And a-vun and a-two… Vay down in Louisiana, down in New Orleans, vay back up in the… Dance my arms faster, Rolf! In not so long ve vill have enuf money for a bag of Berlin's finest heroin."

The Iraq War seems tragic right now, but do you really want America to be so friendly with those guys that they start coming over here and partying with us?

Apart from the Fall Out Boy shirt, Junior HR and JJ Cro-Mags are pretty much 100 percent perfection. Shouldn't Larry Clark be lurking in the background with a camera?

Yes, she's a bit Eurotrashy. But is there anybody alive looking at this that doesn't want to just sink their teeth into her perineum and wave her around in the air like a great white does to a baby seal on Discovery Channel Shark Week?

Sorry ageing fashion guys, but there's nothing fierce about 30 pints of dick cheese fried up in a burning ball of hair.

Uh oh. It's time for the imaginary friends to go to bed or they'll be too sleepy to put ketchup in Dad's coffee tomorrow morning.

KARAOKE

1. Do not hog the mic. If there are three people, you should be singing one-third of the songs. This applies to shy people, too. Don't go to karaoke if you don't want to sing.

2. Pay your way. I don't care how little you sing or how you didn't even want to come out tonight. If you are there for even a minute, you are part of the problem.

3. No slow jams. They are buzzkills.

4. Only sing songs that you actually know. We're not here to watch you try and figure out lyrics. Rap is next to impossible to do, so you better have heard it about 10,000 times before you choose it as a karaoke jam.

5. Sing it as the guy. If you do Prince, try to sound like Prince. If you do Springsteen's "I'm on Fire", you better hoarse up your voice so it sounds right.

6. Only one person on the mic at a time. This is an especially hard rule to follow during Oasis and U2, but sorry dude, that's why there's rules.

He's singing that Bronski Beat classic, "Hey God, What the Fuck Did You Do With My Balls?"

While your friends are going to bars thinking they're heavy shit because they just did seven shots or—ooooh!—they talked to a pretty girl, you are out there, in the streets, destroying society with your bare hands like your life is a Dead Kennedys song.

You might think that the best accessory for the young, attention-seeking homosexual would be a bag or shoes or perhaps a scarf. But you'd be wrong. It's a Filipino midget.

Suicide is for pussies.

You know you're a filthy whore when even your ass is frantically trying to claw its way out of your dress just to get the fuck away from you.

A lot of girls are wearing these long t-shirt dresses that are so short even dogs think, "I wonder if I could get her if she was really wasted and I had coke."

I used to think leg men were fags but every once in a while you see a pair of stems that makes you understand why the 1950s won't shut up about it.

This town ain't big enough for the two of us fucking baby dickhead Scandinavian pussies.

The most satisfying part of asking an ageing male-model Charlie Brown grunge turd to pose for the DOs & DON'Ts is the moment he realises which side of the page he's destined for.

How tranquil and saintly is Jimmy Train Set? I want to be him when I grow up. Actually, can I be him now?

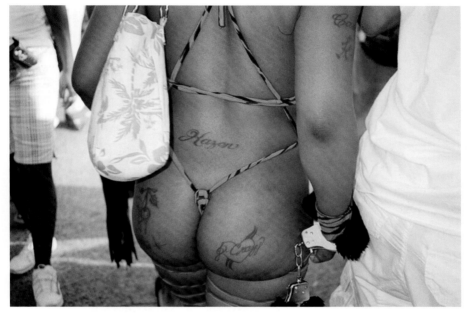

It's nice to get a tattoo of that special someone, unless your life is a revolving door of special someones.

For some reason I always thought that taking him out of the water and putting him in a pair of sweats outside the drug store would divest King Neptune of some of his majesty and grandeur. I was wrong.

Look, nobody's saying you've got to be Brad Pitt to get laid, but when you walk up looking like a lunch box puppet some wizard brought to life for his kid, the sound of vaginas clamping shut is like a machine gun.

You know when you see something in another country with English words written on it that are basically nonsensical because it looks cool, and the person who owns it has no idea what it means? Like a child's backpack in Japan that says "Obama Harry Potter Dragonball Z Brad Pitt"? This car is just like that.

STEALING FROM ENGLISH-AS-A-SECOND-LANGUAGE SPEAKERS Try scowling and saying, "Do you know what I'm talking about?" when you mean "Know what I am saying?" We knew an exchange student who did that, and it ruled. Asking if people want to "make a party" is good too.

 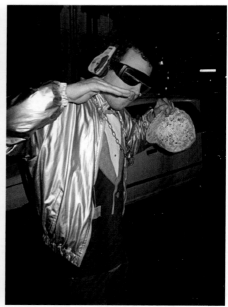

Does anything say "suave eccentric billionaire on holiday" more than a slightly battered vintage briefcase and a perfectly coordinated leisure/flight suit?

Sure, he isn't great friend material if you're lost in Baltimore. But should you be in Paris and need a faggy electro bar where they play Giorgio Moroder and the dad of the girl who owns it built the Pompidou Centre, he's perfect.

Are they wearing those jackets so chicks know what fla-vour of date rape they're going to get? Pink signifies the bewildering, "Did that really happen?" kind and blue means knocked out and waking up on the kitchen floor.

Something inside me wants to molest this Trevor Brown painting come to life but that's a part that I keep buried in the tiny, padlocked box at the bottom of the three-mile-deep closet that's inside another closet that you get to by taking a right turn after skeleton 895 in closet 57.

Hang on a sec, shouldn't you be five inches tall and gyrating on some Hawaiian's dashboard instead of wrecking my ability to get anything done for the rest of the day?

Remember the kid who was a grade ahead of you in junior high who listened to MDC, knew *Watchmen* by heart and smoked pot out of an apple? He hasn't changed at all, and he's still putting the rest of us to shame by not giving one flying fuck.

Why couldn't Dylan Carlson have lent the shotgun to this fey little grunge turd instead? Sure, his sister and mum would cry at the funeral but at least nobody would be stealing their Super Shiny Straightening Serum any more.

If she was a foot shorter this coat would have dramatically different connotations, but right now I'm about 90 percent sure the intended message is, "Why the hell are we driving into Linda's back?"

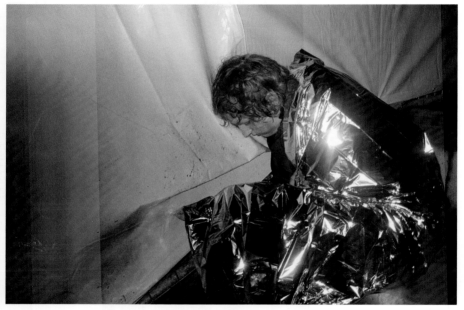

That space blanket is perfect. I want one the next morning that I'm promising God that I'll never do it again as long as I don't die this time.

For those about to double-team the 45-year-old Mexican barback for coke, we salute you.

Hey, you've worked hard all day and if you want to mix yourself a pineapple soda and Popov vodka cocktail on the way home, who's to stop you? The world is your oyster, my friend.

Crazy-eyed bitch leaving you the 33rd voice mail of the night about to heave a brick through your window for never calling her back is a surprisingly good look.

In their spare time, the assistant managers of mobile-phone warehouses stand in car parks wearing jeans designed for 12-year-old girls and making gang signs that mean "free talk time on nights and weekends".

"Look, I ain't gonna make it into work today. My dick exploded."

Oh good. Looks like the pictures finally came back from my future honeymoon.

Heroin hasn't done much for aviation or particle physics lately, but the field of avant-garde hat design is deeply in its debt.

Ah, the independent spirit of the true Parisian male who wears nappies underneath leggings, starts drinking pastis at 8 AM, and never plans on working or making his 1950s bathroom bigger than a matchbox despite the fact that he has a wife and three kids who all live with him, the youngest of which is 28.

Doesn't he look like the giant baby from old Bugs Bunny cartoons? You just want to dab his mouth with one of those scarves then hoist him over your shoulder and say, "Wuh-oh, who made a wittle mess of his food? Who made a wittle mess? Oh, da bad wittle baby made a mess, dat's who!"

BEING A MAN Men are not allowed to wear any kind of baby-carrying knapsack. A kid only weighs 30 pounds, and if you can't carry that, you're not much of a dad. Men's bikes cannot have baskets, and men cannot wear helmets. Actually, neither gender can wear bike helmets, not even messengers. What is with this obsession with safety, anyways? Does your mummy follow you around kvetching in your ear about how dangerous everything is? Men cannot wear overalls or mittens or anything that a kid would wear. Men cannot pay more than £10 for a haircut, and ideally would just do it at home with a pair of clippers. If it takes you more than 15 minutes to get ready, you are a fag.

First of all, that better not be his kid. Secondly, don't own an earth-toned BabyBjörn and expect not to get searched at the airport, Cheech. I can smell your dank nuggets from a mile away.

The best way to guarantee no one ever breaks into your trailer is to combine the two things that civilisation has, throughout history, been most afraid of: pirates (hence the Jolly Roger) and working-class people (hence the Burberry). Nobody would dare fly a plane into this thing, much less try to burglarise it while the owners are at the bar drinking pints of black Sambuca and beating their children with spiked bats.

You know what, you fucking idiot? We're glad you're dead. We're glad the last image your friends have of you is skating down the stairs dressed as a Thai cowboy and then lying there bug-eyed like a Matthew Barney sculpture that haemorrhaged from too many blow jobs.

Used to be a dad like this would have the kid in therapy at age 10. These days divorce and addiction in the family are so common that kids are just like, "Meh, fuck this loser. Who wants to go spend what I just stole from his wallet?"

Guy, you may as well be wearing a t-shirt that says "Clowns Touched My Area When I Was Five".

There's a new style of tit job in town. They're calling it the "Beverly Hills Quarter Pounder With Cheese".

I have a feeling that if this was the guy who came to fix the office computers we'd never have that problem with the fucking email ever again.

I was sad because I had no shoes, then I saw a guy who had folded two pot-leaf-emblazoned pieces of attic insulation over his feet and tied them with Scotch tape and I was like, "Wait, what the fuck is going on with that guy?"

Some people pretend they've never watched *Nathan Barley* while others embrace the fact that they're smug, spoiled, wisecracking dickheads and make the most of it.

Whenever some old fart starts bitching about how Korea is America's "forgotten war", it just makes us think of our nation's real unappreciated heroes: the veterans of the TransXanthian Star-Incident on Rigel VII.

Dance like nobody's watching. Love like you've never been hurt. Sing like nobody's listening. Fall asleep in a children's playground with a fully loaded high-powered handgun on your belt.

Newsflash to the single guys who pay for festival tickets as soon as they're announced. The devil finally made a rape kit you can fit in your back pocket!

DOs

Dragged away screaming is still obviously the industry standard, but we think led spacily by the arm with a sliver of jizz on your chin has a refined sense of debauched insouciance that could make it a real competitor this year.

You've got to be out of your mind to commit suicide by tiger.

"Heeeyyyy you guyysss were awwwessome. I've been coming to this place every single night for 15 yearssh and you remind me of the first time I saw Oasshhsishh. Do you have a PR? I can be your PR girl. I know Courtney Love. Hey wait! Where are you going? Come back!"

Curious couple seeks like-minded individuals for discreet fun and games. Genuine photos a must. No time wasters!

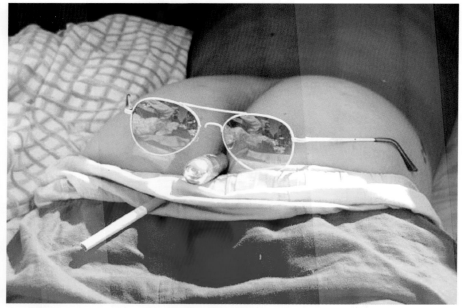

All those ad agencies were right. Cigarettes and shades can make any asshole look like a totally cool dude.

SMOKES Always let people bum smokes, no matter how many you have left. It is a fucking cigarette, and it's the principle of the thing we're talking about here.

Sorry to the rich kids with sailor tattoos and Born Against t-shirts from eBay, but nobody does "ABC No Rio Relic" better than alcoholic teenagers from San Francisco who just found a jump rope in the alley.

Oh good, it looks like the direct ferry service from the Island of Dr Moreau to central Paris is up and running again. That's a relief.

She looks like an undiscovered species of lemur.

"Those jocks down in AR may think they can push me around and hide my trackball and move my purchase orders to the back of the queue, but they can't touch me now. This is Brian's time to shiiiiiiine!"

DOs

Sure, the Dominican Republic is the North American hub for human trafficking, but look where it's got them. If you had such a fuckable national resource, wouldn't you want to sell off some of the surplus too?

Tommy Chong's been a bit hard to handle since moving to Japan, but honestly, we're just happy to see him enjoying his golden years to their fullest.

This woman can see your future, and your future is having your balls glued to a 747 that's flying into an 80-storey disco.

Not trying to sound queer or nothing, but how are regular girls supposed to compete with this? They should be thanking God every day for remembering to put vaginas in their crotches.

How come every after-hours drug party at some random loft these days is filled with predatory old queens who offer you bumps of rohypnol and claim it's coke? Aren't these guys supposed to be dead?

"Mum, where's Dad?" "I don't know, Julian. He said he was just going to get us a bottle of water."

It took years of searching and millions of pounds in private-eye fees and plane tickets, but we finally found the secret store where all the DON'Ts get their clothes. (It's in China, by the way.)

Shovelling snow off the steps of your parents' house is about as metal as two dolphins jumping over a rainbow and tongue kissing.

Is the one on the right levitating or has all the blood in my eyes and brain just bolted for my dick?

Drinking whiskey out of the bottle in the middle of a foreign city at midnight is pretty much the ultimate DO of boozing. Not only does it make you sing great and say really funny stuff that never offends anybody, but it also has the power to get you laid with male models.

Willy the Vampire Slayer here knows that it's not just garlic that nightwalkers fear. A greasy, matted fake fur jacket that looks like my grandmother's carpet is also anathema to the undead.

We're not saying mums should be stuck in the kitchen cooking all day, but when your pierced genitals are dragging on the street and your fucking feedbags are hanging out of your leather jacket it may be time to take it down a notch.

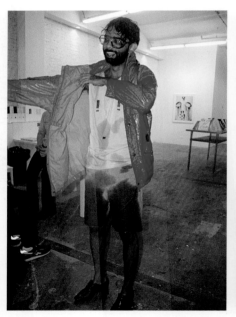 

If you'd have said, "Imagine a nu-rave Pakistani nerd who looks like he's pissed himself at an art gallery," I never would have dreamed it'd be somebody I'd want to go for a beer with.

Maybe a smidgen too much emotional honesty for the first date, but the sooner we get our foibles out into the open, the more we can love each other unconditionally forever and ever.

Haven't we told you people before that nobody over the age of 35 should be wearing trainers?

DOs

Waking up in a bar with a black man's dick in your face is only a good look if you passed out with it in your mouth. Otherwise it's a little too frat house.

Coke-bloat guys with lots of theories about Peter Sotos get boring after hour two, but they've always got shit-loads of coke on them.

Q: What do you get when you cross *Absolutely Fabulous* with 30-something Ministry groupies?
A: Two clammy-skinned old bats with more emotional issues than the entire population of Arkham Asylum.

Are you so immersed in the new Yeasayer or whatever the fuck it is that you have gone into a pursed-lip, closed-eye reverie waiting for the train? Why isn't someone braining you with a bottle and taking all your shit?

MUSIC Don't talk about music. Nobody cares what you listen to. It's nice that the Clash "changed your life", but save it for your grandkids. The one exception to this rule is a bit of nerding out if you are up at 5 AM coking out to records. Even in that situation, however, use music talk sparingly.

It's a DJ's job to start trends and if that trend is making your hair look like an Irish girl's cunt then so be it. Don't stand in the way of progress.

This guy has been into AC/DC so long he's on their seventh wave of irony.

Wikipedia is now available as a drinking buddy that folds up into your pocket when you're done asking him stuff.

You've got to be the unluckiest photographer in the world to be facing the wrong way when an atom bomb goes off.

What a sturdy set of wheels. I bet if you crashed that into the back of a mystery white Fiat in a Parisian underpass all the occupants would totally survive.

After spending several months making her hair look like a homeless man's, she had her trousers professionally pissed for £2,000.

"Boo-fucking-hoo. You lost out to a toucan as the face of Froot Loops. Get over it and move on already because seriously, Phil, we are sick of hearing you whine."

If the music industry doesn't want to collapse by June they should hire more guys like this. They'd come free with Neil Young reissues and visit your house with some weed and an eightball every time you played *Tonight's the Night*.

We try to avoid putting up photos that have shitty res, but we're making an exception for this snap of one guy eating out another guy's asshole, captured at 10 AM on a weekday by a reader in Australia. We're not even going to try to make a cute comment here. Just look at it. Behold it.

I hope they're still taking proposals for the new World Trade Center design so we can nominate this kid.

This is what the world would look like if more time travellers set their sights on gangster rap instead of baby Hitler.

There's a fine line between horny-slob-who's-up-for-it in a good, old-fashioned fuck-in-the-bathroom way and horny-slob-who's-up-for-it in a Jesus-Christ-what-have-I-done, gonorrhoea-ish way.

I guess fashion is vital and art and stuff, but it also allows for "shoots" that are all about 30 people helping one person take photos of a 16-year-old anorexic giraffe from Estonia.

The best thing about giving up booze for a couple of months isn't the better sleep or the lack of hangovers or saving money. It's having a wee sip of your first drink of the new year and it being so fucking delicious you want to pop your eyeballs out of your head so you can drink them as well.

The odds of getting two girls back to your place after a night of boozing is very low. The odds of a threesome going down are way lower. But if you don't at least bust out a "Why don't you guys make out?" your wank Rolodex will hate you for the rest of its life.

It takes a real man to admit that he's wrong and an even realer man to gather up his druthers, pick up some flowers, and head over there to apologise. Let's do this, Howard.

DOs

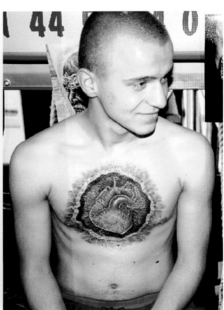

Close your eyes and try to think of the absolute lamest activity you can. What did you come up with? WRONG. It's shopping for patches at a flea market. Collecting and buying funky patches is like taking out a restraining order against seeing a respectable vagina.

My new tattoo means "Somebody put a cigar out on my distended anus and then I drew a heart in it".

Vrum, vrum, vrubububububababam eeeeeeeerrmrummrumm eeeeeeeeeeeeeeeer-huhmeeeeeeeeeeeeeee eeeeeeer-rr- huhmeeeeeeeeeeeeeerr-ERRRRRRRRRRRRRRK!

If American kids are really serious about bringing back skinhead they need to spend a little less time arguing about Harringtons versus bombers and just focus on getting down the basics.

SHOPPING The secret to buying clothes is to have your look totally figured out before you walk into the shop. That's how the mods did it. Fred Perry, Ben Sherman, bowling shoes, loafers and parkas. If they saw a great pair of baggy cords, too bad, it's not mod (no matter what Madness say about trousers). You need to do that too. Is she going for rich hippy? OK, that means only really expensive shoes, flowing summer dresses, and the odd tassled leather jacket. Want some free black leather Converse? No, you don't, because that's not rich hippie. What about a vintage Judas Priest shirt? Nope. But if after a year or two she decides she's going for a Cheech & Chong theme, stumbling across some leather Converse and a Judas Priest shirt becomes a blessing. The key to this whole philosophy is to be able to say no to a total score. If you're going for preppy prick and you see an amazing pair of Lemmy cowboy boots that fit you perfectly, you have to walk away. Shopping is about staying focused and keeping your eye on the prize!

Oh dear Lord. Look how soft and unspoiled she is. Too bad you're on your way to a party where the girl you drunkenly cheated on her with last week is definitely going to be. Why do girlfriends only ever look this good when you're engulfed in a flaming pillar of regret?

Beam me up a £30 blowjob, Scotty! The Swedish Vulcan rent boys have landed and they're draining gallery owners' balls like Roto-Rooter on crank.

Is this guy modelling for the Dads That Never Do Anything That Doesn't Annoy the Living Shit Out of You memorial?

Word of advice to all the 20-year-old virgins. Take care of those blue balls before they take care of you.

Something about the combination of muscular skinhead thug and delicately flavoured rabbit tagliatelle in a beautiful back garden in Rome is making me ask myself that age-old question again: Am I a fag?

If you're six-foot-ten and you find yourself at a daytime rave dressed as a giant alien with mascara running down your face, it may finally be time to stop listening to your unconditionally supportive friends and family and seriously consider taking your own life.

When you're 250 lbs of pure muscle you can dress like a total asshole and get away with it. It's in the Asshole Constitution. Look it up.

Older chicks rule because their apartments are always clean, they know how to cook a nice meal and they are super-grateful when you eat them out.

Can you imagine being this guy's pubes?

She's the personification of the razor bumps women get around their holes. She's human vag-lip burn.

In my dreams she's a superhero called Bubbles and she has the ability to kill her enemies with giant blobs of banana custard shot out of her asshole.

Living historians are cool because they cut through all the boring textbook shit and get straight to the real dirt you want to learn about, like Lincoln's gay lovers or Ben Franklin's colossal gunt.

It's time to stop eating the hash cakes for breakfast when every single muscle in your face is straining upwards to keep your eyes open.

Oh good, the dry heaves I ordered just got here.

We've been trying to contact the guys in the Paris office for over a week now, but nobody can get hold of them. If anybody has any clues, drop us a line.

How come ageing East Village vets always have this smirky, "Seen it all" demeanour even though "it all" can usually be summed up as the same barback's decaying pussy once every couple of months?

Burkas are mean and women's rights are good and blah blah blah. But if you were rape-married to the Saudi Gomer Pyle, you'd be pulling this thing over your head with a huge sigh of relief every time he dragged you out in public too.

In Stockholm he's a legendary performance artist from the 60s who all the punk kids call "Grandfather Martin". In New York he's a scary bum who's about to take a shit in the middle of the train and then stab you with his four-inch fingernails.

You think you're tired of all the novelty moustaches running around these days? Imagine what it's like for the leather fags they stole it from in the first place.

For Spanish tourists in New York, every single shitty boring square inch of sidewalk is "super fantastic". Can you imagine how hard their minds would be blown if it was actually still fun here?

Sure, old rockers never die, but it's also true that the only pussy they get is from deluded middle-aged Dutch crusties with hair that smells like wet dog and clammy ass cheeks hanging out of labia-strangling leather shorts like doughballs with not enough yeast in them.

DRUGS If you aren't at work, smoke weed whenever you want. But you are not allowed to go around telling everyone how stoned you are. That's for 13-year-olds.

We've said before, no bumps of coke after 4:30 AM.

Prior to age 25, it is OK to have one night of dabbling with heroin every six months. After 25, no more getting down with the brown. You'll just look like a gross old junkie the next day. You can switch to pills for your every-six-months opiate indulgence until you have kids. Then you never get to relax again until you're a senior citizen.

Don't worry about me, Dad. I'm alone in another city with writing on my tits that asks strangers to give me drugs.

Now that we have Grim Reaper 2.0, I can't wait to die.

Today the people who invent stuff look like Craig and Johnny or whatever their names are from YouTube, but in the 1800s inventors strolled about looking like this, chucking orphans into the Thames for fun.

Guys who actually think with their dicks can be pretty rough on the eyes (and ears and nose and brains and fists), but they've got nothing on the girls who think with guys' dicks.

This picture seems like a DO slam dunk until you take into account the v-neck-to-tuxedo-vest-to-champagne combo move and also the part where you realise his name is Garrett, he shaves his pubes and he refers to sex with a woman as "tackling a slampig".

You don't need cutting-edge fashion blogs to key you into what look is in this summer, because this guy already nailed it. Rick Moranis dressed as a Nepalese Sherpa.

You thought she'd left but she's only ditched her friends and come back upstairs and now you are definitely going to fuck her tonight. This is how people marooned in shark-infested waters feel when they see the helicopters coming to save them.

 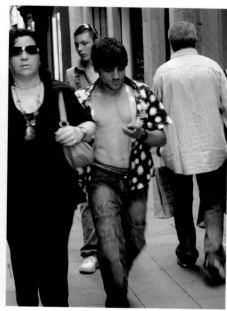

"Umbrella" was a great song but they need to give Rihanna a rest from the TV appearances or we're going to end up with another Britney situation.

I always thought "gigolo whose phone is ringing off the hook" would look a lot better than this.

A tear filled my eye as I watched this lovely old bat nobly hobbling off to the patisserie. Why don't they make people as good as this anymore? Maybe we should have some more world wars.

I've got no clue what homos are planning to do with marriage once they've got the go-ahead, but considering the tan-creamed, Malibu-Barbie tumour we've let it become, they've got their work cut out for them.

DOs

While you were sitting on the couch squandering the weekend watching the *Deadliest Catch* marathon, this is what was happening down at the lake.

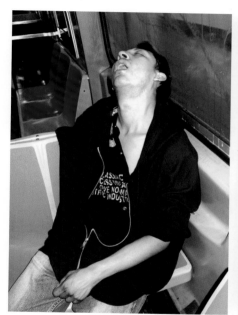

If you really had balls you'd stick one of them in this guy's mouth.

Wow, it's the entire spectrum of Worst Guys. Everything from the drunk yuppie millionaire at the wedding to the nu-metal rave-goth demanding change.

Painful at first maybe, but after applying Human Haemorrhoid Remover
my asshole feels brand-spankingly, sparklingly, tingly-tangily new.

Here's the reason why in 10 years time your mobile phone/whole life will be a computer chip in your asshole: so spoiled little goblins like Prajit will only have to fart to tell the internet to change their profile pictures.

DOs

The sooner children accept that life is hell and we've all got to get through it alone, the better. If that means dragging the kid out in a blizzard and leaving it to fend for itself, so be it. One day the little whelp will show up on your doorstep and thank you.

Fuck what the kid thinks. If you got some trim last night, let that flag fly.

FAMILY The second you ejaculate into a woman, you have to start thinking about how you're going to pay for its education. If your parents don't happily pay for all your education, they are stupid gaylords. No matter how poor you are. They're also supposed to help you start a business and pay for the wedding and help you buy a house. Of course, once they get too old to live normally, you have to take them in. Old-age homes are not cool.

Gay black teenagers are the best people in the entire world. They are always the funniest, the meanest, and the most-est talented at some goddamn thing. Sweeping generalisation? Well, fuck it, it's true.

So is camel-toe pride her whole deal? If so, we're getting in line to get a photo with her too.

Swedish bums have too much money and healthcare to elicit any sympathy, so feel free to yell, "Move it, Clogs," and send this guy careening into the flowers.

"Hello Gothenburg! We're The Deluded Fucking Assholes and this one's about being unable to keep up your child support payments."

Have you ever noticed how often girls with big areolas tend to be more or less completely out of their fucking minds?

Bony boy chest inside a boilersuit is anathema to all that is classically feminine and—whoops! My dick just ripped up the rule book.

Does playing bass really make anyone sweat that much? Put your shirt back on, Frenchy. You aren't a bricklayer.

Isn't it weird to still see Uggs, flip-flops and Crocs? It's almost as if everyone in the world isn't reading the DOs & DON'Ts and giving a shit what we think.

If they really want more of us to join the army, they should just pay her to travel to bars signing us up while we're drunk. It would work a lot better than those commercials where soldiers are being screamed at in the dark while driving a jeep over a cliff.

An *On the Waterfront* vibe is always a strong look, but a bandage from somebody trying to break a beer bottle on your head the night before makes it titanium-plated.

As much as we want to like Teddy boys for de-fagging mod, we just can't shake the fact they look like someone combined a homeless production of *Bye Bye Birdie* with the opposite of a beauty pageant.

I'm not sure which is worse anymore: trying to use a computer so shitty it falls apart the second you put a CD in it, or being forced to take part in a bunch of one-love bullshit that's even gayer than the Dalai Lama's anal beads.

With Iggy Pop advertising car insurance and the Sex Pistols sticking their name on whatever it is this month that they're sticking their name on, it's nice to see that Patti Smith isn't afraid to take music back to the streets.

The only thing worse than an 18-year-old boy is a 22-year-old boy. Look at their slimy man-child faces, awkwardly smoking cigars and ordering grown-up drinks that they don't know the ingredients of. We had to get out of there before they started telling us how "mad crazy" the recession is.

Maybe there's something in the water in Mumbai (besides raw sewage), but Indian kids are having higher and earlier cuteness peaks than white kids. Sorry, baby Parvati—it's all downhill from here.

I love the folks who think you can actually fill kids' brains with a bunch of stuff about respecting differences and avoiding stereotypes, as if the second they're out the door they aren't playing basketball-rappers and Santa-Jedis at Abu Ghraib.

I'm sure there's something more to be said about this photo, but I still can't get past the fact that there's someone out there who has to cut the feet off their socks to make them fit.

When the ball connected with the paddle, the feet lifted slightly off the sand and the garlic-scented scrotum jiggled upwards, bouncing briefly between the pimply buttocks and the vinegary penis. Who's hungry?

STRIP CLUBS Your boyfriend is allowed to go to a strip club once a week. After that, it gets weird. Also, if you're only getting fucked when he's been out to strip clubs all night, it's a sign of something very bad. If he adheres to the once-a-week rule, he is allowed to get lap dances and champagne room and whatever he wants. Just don't talk about it.

Future wives of Russian mobsters are schooled for a life of servility and lying to the cops by being force-fed cocaine and having to dance half nude in nightclubs from the age of 12. Here we see one of this rare breed about two years away from graduation.

Well, here's a novel solution to the whole "jocks versus nerds" dilemma. Just cram them both on the same hot girl and call it a day.

How about that glorious period called 18-to-20 when you stumble from party to party reeking of sex and booze and all you have to worry about is where you left the number of the girl who gave you ketamine last night or whenever it was.

I wonder how tough guy here would feel if he knew how many gay dudes are going to jerk off to this photo.

Dear Cheryl, homo stylists make Agyness Deyn's hair like that so men won't find her attractive any more. And they use qualified hairdressers too. You look like *When Something About Mary Met King Kong*.

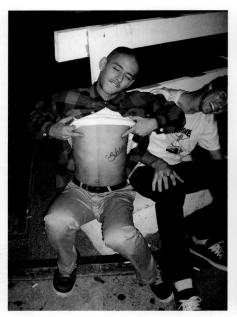

Does it make me gay if I just want to confirm that he's got a nice healthy cock underneath those shiny new Dickies?

The only thing wrong with this guy's outfit is his ashy knees. Still, the question remains: How did he escape the eightsome?

I would fuck my name off that guestlist.

"Son, I admire how shitty you've been acting recently but if you really want to make it in this world you've got to get your priorities right and knuckle down if you want to be anywhere near as terribly fucking atrociously awful as I am when you're my age."

DOs

It's hard to call out your friends on their bullshit without it seeming like a joke, but if one of them is turning into a serious, self-important asshole it's vital to figure out a way to slip him the news.

When gay terrorists blow themselves up they get this instead of the standard 72 virgins.

When one girl in the room understands the merits of squishing her pudge around, everyone else can dress like Frankenstein and give it up to anyone who asks, they're still invisible.

This is the only time a black dude has ever worn 15 pounds of baby toys and a Hitler moustache to the same rave, and that's amazing. Find a chubby white girl with neon dreadlocks to give him head.

And here we have the only thing less manly than sleeping in the park—hopping on the swing set and gleefully going to and fro. You just had to feel the breeze caress your wrinkles, huh?

Sure I get PMT, but never that bad that anybody notices.

That Starbucks salad and coffee cost around $10. Four of those and she would have had her "ticket". Fifty of them and she could afford the abortion.

Oh look. It's a production still from the new season of *Black Dudes Fuck the Darndest White Ladies*.

Will somebody please pass me a magnum of champagne so that I might christen the USS Ass Worship?

It may not seem fair but some ladies just have an inborn regality, and that's something all the Valium in the world can't take away.

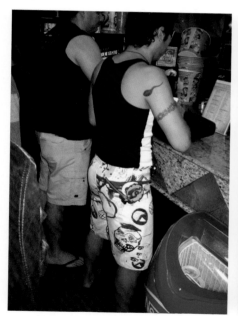

OK, so you see sperms as tiny party animals or whatever—fine. Did it not occur to you for even one second that you have a permanent tattoo of cum on your back?

How can you go wrong with a couple of cherry balls on your face and the teeth of a homeless man from 1604? Well, two broken purses and a penis is a good start.

Right on! If those fucking snack narcs think they can get between you and some delicious frozen treats right now, they're gonna get what's coming to them. You are totally in control of this situation!

She's a DO as in "I'd like to DO things to you and make you use your outside voice while I'm inside you", but also a DON'T as in "you DON'T have any style and your outfit has the sex appeal of a school-bus fire".

There's a special place in hell for people who use animals as fashion accessories. It's a few caves over from lawyers and right below beauty-pageant parents.

Are biker ex-hippies so over everything that their whole life is just kidding, or does four decades of pot turn your brain into an eight-year-old impressionist from Versailles who shits the bed and has no friends?

Most supermodels are stupid, boring Aryan cunts. But what about when they look like Miles Davis reincarnated in the body of the new female Antichrist whose mission is to destroy all DON'Ts? We're fastidiously matching our socks to our shirts so maybe she'll stop staring at us like that.

As cool as it would be to have telekinesis, you know there'd be no way to keep your brain under control when a girl like this walks up with her top held together by one stressed out button.

VOGUE, ETC. Don't read fashion magazines at all. Poor Mary Kate Olsen, she's anorexic. Poor Karen Carpenter, she died. Fashion magazines are for the girls you hated in school. All of them—*Vogue*, *Bazaar*, *Elle*—are forced to use the clothing provided by their advertisers. That's how they get the ads, which is how they get the money to pay for Kate Moss and her cocaine. All of those magazines are basically just one big ad, and for ugly fucking clothes usually, too.

This is the Yorkshire version of blowing out candles on a birthday cake. You drink your age in cans of cheap lager and then burn off your chest hair trying to blow out the camp fire.

If that guy on the left keeps photo-bombing this efficiently, I'm gonna be out of a job.

This lil' weirdo likes being attacked by dogs so much he dressed himself up as a chew toy.

You were 99.9 percent of the way there and then... WAW WAMP WAAAMMMMP you sink the whole thing into the ocean with those fucking old-lady-in-Miami-Beach shoes. What is it with you people and your terrible footwear choices?

Escaped Russian-convict gypsy-sex-cult members who bum little boys for breakfast are the best people to base your next tattoo on.

Remember when Ja Rule was the biggest rapper in "the game"? What the fuck was that about?

Girls who know how to do olde-timey lingerie without making it some 1940s cosplay bullshit are basically boner Valkyries.

The best thing about kids who are raised in Williamsburg is that they know firsthand how boring creative white people are. They didn't have to learn it from a blog like the rest of us.

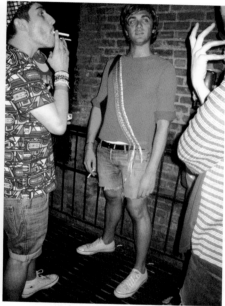

She spent so long getting ready, she rolled over the line that separates "made up" from "in drag".

Who knew someone's posture could be so infuriating? Are we *All Aboard! Rosie's Family Cruise* and the boat is tipping sideways? Somebody please rip off those orthopaedic legs and give them back to their rightful owner.

How much of a better trip would it be if you bought your drugs off this guy rather than some fat college kid who doesn't even bother looking up from his Xbox?

Isn't it weird that anytime a meathead/frat-boy-type character who wears football jerseys and Jägermeister keychain necklaces tries to be funny or zany, he always ends up looking like a cartoon rapist from outer space?

This guy looks like he was designed by a brilliant Japanese minimalist like Shigeo Fukuda. Just when the hoes, the beer and the tattoo were getting too much he pulls it back with matching black, some leggy shorts, and girls' slip-ons.

He may be a bit chubby for heroin chic but not everyone can pull off Clark Kent as JT Leroy if he played guitar for the Sonics.

This is fine at a Dickinson College football game, but when it's on your back in public you end up making your asshole look like a fucking asshole (like, literally, an asshole that's used for fucking).

They might make you look like a shamelessly lazy fat pig, but these things are great for catching up with the ice-cream van.

COMPLICATED TATTOOS Honestly, we'd rather you just get a sick Tasmanian Devil caged in tribal bars with a voice-bubble full of Chinese symbols than listen to your story about how this particular sacred heart with a sword on the side symbolises this really tough time in your life and how looking at it in the mirror every morning truly makes you realise how far you've come.

When you put a tramp stamp of a weeping child-angel on your unshirted back, you're basically taking out a restraining order against ovaries.

All those evangelicals who think you can deprogramme gays are fucking idiots, and to prove it I am going to try to "deprogramme" my heterosexuality by giving this guy hand jobs for the rest of his life (watch, it won't work).

Wouldn't it be awesome if, instead of hiding it, your teacher went, "That's right kids. I munch on dinks like they're a box of Yodels©. Now let's move on and learn our black asses some fucking geography!"

People who think riding their bicycle is saving the world and vocalists dressed in vintage-store garbage need to all move to an island somewhere where they can worship each other as much as they want. Oh wait, they did, it's called Williamsburg.

If you're sure you've perfected invisible spray why not try it out at home with a friend first, especially when your body is a Frankenstein compilation of about 36 different bodies?

You know what? If you're cute—go cute. Tattoos and facial scars look ridiculous on human figurines, so get your shit from a toy store and stand there until we tickle you within an inch of your life.

We were at an intellectual dinner party discussing how impossible it is to be fierce in the winter when this girl came out of the bathroom and said, "Oh yeah?" and everyone was like, "Wha?" and she was all, "Check it" and we we're like, "No you did not!" and she's all, "What? Are you blind?" and we were all, "Oh shit!"

You could have been a contender but no, you had to pop that on your head. Dude, quirky hats are for kids' toys and fun grandmas dying of breast cancer.

Oh look, a rodeo clown had to get dressed up for a funeral. What died, his chances of getting any girl with an IQ over 100?

That thing about black farts being good luck may be true and it may be bullshit. Why not err on the side of caution however and capture at least one of them in your favourite t-shirt?

LA is so warm and easy and greasy you can almost smell the balls the second you get out of the airport.

When Australian girls saw videos of No Pants Day in New York, instead of going "Ha," they said, "Bluff called." Now everyone is in permanent morning-after-sex mode with wads of cash and spare sunglasses shoved down the back of their underwear, and the only thing keeping the forest of boners down are the omni-present flip-flops.

Why are uncles so much cooler than dads? Oh yeah, uncles didn't spend a quarter of a century with you up in their grill making them bald and shitty.

Dear ladies, picking your zits until your face looks like it slept in rats is like smooch repellent only scarier.

Sorry but the tuxedo-and-Chucks thing is for the zany guy at the prom who wears Vuarnets on a string and has one chocolate bar up each sleeve.

Now that the skinheads are gone it's time to rifle through their leftovers and take the best parts. Doc Martens are still a no-no and we don't need the bleach splatters or the shaved heads but what about just the middle part? Yes? All right!

Suspenders on girls and those Judi Rosen-type jeans that go up to your ribs are so regal yet goofy it's like fucking around with the princess of architecture.

The winter hat indoors is only a little worse than sunglasses but BAPE? When did models start dressing like suburban wiggers who use Wii nunchucks and say "Get crunked"?

If you like to wear grunge pyjamas but you can't get laid in New York or London, move to Nebraska and hang out at art galleries, where the one pretty girl in town will be forced to talk to you.

A massive influx of Asians into North America has forced white girls to raise the cute bar to just above pubescent, which is a real bummer if you're not a heterosexual male with a healthy libido.

After a lifetime of compliments, pretty girls get dressed with such grace and good sense each morning it's like a Christo and Jeanne-Claude project.

What is with this David Copperfield bathing-suit bullshit where women create the illusion of being nude? Fuck off, peekaboo hips.

Even though it tastes delicious, crack should be avoided at all costs. Addicts spend their whole lives searching for the higher high, often moving on from inhaling crack to injecting it into their necks to spontaneously burying their faces deep inside any crack they can find. Such as this one.

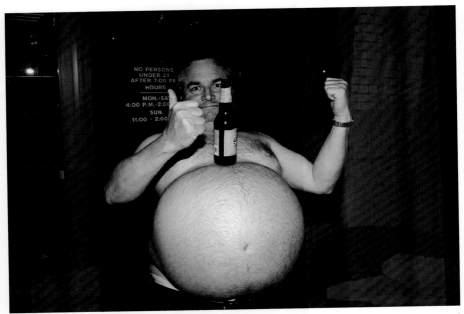

Just before Neil Armstrong got back into his spacecraft, he chugged a beer, threw the bottle into a crater, and said, "Moon, you da man!"

DRINKING Ideally, men only drink beer. That way, when you are kind enough to get a round, you don't have a bunch of LA faggots saying, "I'll have a raspberry vodka with a splash of Citron and a fucking lime" or whatever. How are we supposed to remember five woman drinks? "Five Buds for five buds" is all we should have to remember.

Women, on the other hand, can drink whatever the fuck they want. They look like fun tomboys when they drink beer and they look like classy broads when they drink Tom Collins, so the whole spectrum is great news (go bananas).

DOs

It's still summer in Australia and everyone's dressing like a fat Japanese girl that's sleeping at your house because her dad found her dildo and he is fucking furious but she couldn't give a shit and she's not falling for his tyrannical bullshit anymore.

"Hey, Grandpa Leduc, what did you do in the early 2000s?" "Well, Jean-Marc, me and my friends drove to America and followed around some band that was named after cum."

DOs

The only thing better than a girl turning a sweatshirt and jeans into something more heavy-shit than lingerie is said girl asking you if you want to come inside.

Matching couples used to be a DON'T no-brainer, but when you look this clean we forget about the rules and dream of eating shrimp off your genitalia.

Call me an asshole but people who like to be pissed on are pieces of shit. Actually, shit doesn't even like being pissed on. It just allows it because that's life when you're shit.

Is this what narcs look like nowadays? They can't wear jean jackets with Zoso on the back, so now you have old dudes with "rare trainers", "counterculture" blazers, high-end denim, articulated knees and Offspring dreads coming up to you and asking if there's any place around here to "score some 'erb".

You know when you go home to visit your parents and they get boring around ten, so you go out to see what your old high school buddies are doing these days and the party is so weird and fun you catch yourself thinking, "Wait a minute. Why the fuck did I ever leave this town?"

For the last fucking time: men cannot have hairdos. Men cannot walk into salons and sit in those big chairs and lean back into a sink while a rich cokehead makes a £200 sculpture on their head. All women know this. That's why they do this look when you take a picture.

Oh Lord in heaven above. The way those socks and shoes work together and the way her knee playfully peeks out of her skirt. I'm dicknotised.

We have no idea what's going on here and it's kind of freaking us out, but we'd rather be scared than bored so bring it on.

When someone is this clueless it actually gets kind of scary. Like the way a lot of serial killers are autistic and they don't look people in the eye because they don't get what the big deal is with eyes.

Ten years ago, if you saw somebody with a Misfits shirt you could guarantee at least ten minutes of "something in common" conversation with them. These days you just drop your shit and run in case they pull out a Mossberg and start shooting all their classmates.

Not sure if this is racist of me or God, but why don't white crazies approach their mental illness with this level of flair? Is it the centuries of having to make lemonade out of lemons or is there something in melanin that kicks in when the rest of the brain shuts down and crowns you King Sofa the Third.

Imagine spending a month's pay on a beach holiday to find this guy in your face every morning for a week, his pleated camo miniskirt just high enough to constantly remind you how many times his scout-troop leader fingered him.

PUBLIC SHITTING If you smell a bad shit come out of your ass, start flushing immediately. There is no limit to the number of courtesy flushes allowed. Also, you have to give the next guy a heads-up. Because once that poor bastard goes in there after you, he can't just come running out screaming (like he wants to), because then you're all embarrassed and it's a weird vibe all around the restaurant. Just a little eye roll or gesture should do the job—be subtle but clear.

This shit is gay.

She kept trying to tell us it was OK because "it's tradee-tional" but I don't know of any culture that's cool with shitting in public.

DOs

When nerds gave up pocket protectors and became greasy metalheads we picked up their glasses and went, "Hey, these are awesome!" Now the nerds are angry (cue Nelson Muntz).

If any of you are ever editing a psychology text book and need a photo for the "depression" chapter, I feel this sums it up pretty tidily.

You might think you're a big fan of Chicken Pussy, but this guy just put you to fucking shame.

Going to Europe and seeing people under 30 who don't look like they're wearing drugstore GG Allin costumes is such an ocular relief it's like shooting Valium into your eyes.

Girls with guns are fucking hot and they give all guys a bulge in the front of their trousers, but when she's in Israel things get real dark real fast and the bulge ends up coming out the back of our trousers instead.

If this is what DJs who still use vinyl and "keep it real" look like, I'll stick with model/actress getting paid comical amounts of money to futz around on her iPod, thank you.

Notice his bummed-out, dumbfounded expression? He just remembered how many manatees died in the last minute because of pollution. I hope this dude gets decapitated by a Frisbee or drowns in a gravity bong.

Finally some body-positive pioneers have broken the horniness barrier and proven that it's just as easy for men to be sultry, graceful water nymphs as bulbous Foghorn Leghorns with zit-covered thighs and constant gas.

If you have five daughters and you see this kid threatening to kill people with his giant plastic sword, it will snap your heart in two. Look away.

This look (usually with an army jacket) has become a uniform for all East Coast pretty girls and if that's boring then I love being boring more than Al Gore.

Sure, they've banned smoking in public places, but when are they gonna ban blowing douche bubbles?

How perturbed and uncomfortable does he look with his sad attempt at "weird guy"? Face it, buddy: You're normal. Strap on a white baseball cap and a J. Crew button-down and call it a day.

DOs

As you can see, understanding the basic elements of design is crucial to a good look. Of course, the former does not guarantee the latter as can be seen with the brown-nyloned Japanese and the socks-and-sandalled Germans.

If God has blessed you with his own image from the waist up you might not want to blow it from the waist down by becoming a lesbian contractor.

Funny when you're 15. Fucking futile when you're 40.

DOs

Bums are a bummer because they can't hold it together but when crazy people have some cash and can handle their meds they make the party something to believe in.

This is what the world would be like if you could make girls' jeans invisible and stare at their strange bruises.

"Look, you got the Smash Mouth CDs I sent, my niece taught you about the slang—what are you worried about? Everything's going to be fine. Now get in there and find out who their supplier is. Over."

Most ladies like it when their boyfriends are at least a little possessive, but making her wear a You suit goes way past class rings and letter jackets into some serious Phil Spector territory.

Basing your entire look around being surprised to see me is so flattering you might as well be dressed as a morning blowjob.

Trying to argue this situation into a DON'T is harder than masturbating to *Roseanne*.

Homeless! Wait, hip! No no, homeless! Hip?! Fuck it.

She's a streetwalkin' cheetah with a bag full of tofu burgers and half-used jars of hemp seed ointment to wax the beard she's growing out of her asshole.

Now that the Horrors have taught clever, gothic nerds how to dress without looking like they're about to mutilate school kids with pipe bombs, these once-stay-at-homers are getting more pussy than Dracula.

God bless the party martyrs like Carl on the right up there. Taking him to the hospital to get his stomach pumped because he almost choked on his own vomit after chugging a pint of vodka may be a pain in the ass now, but it will one day become the stuff of friend folklore.

COOL KIDS You should not say "cool kids", especially if by "cool kids" you mean people you admire and respect who won't talk to you because you suck. But even if you mean something else, don't say "cool kids".

If there's nothing going on tonight don't sit on your ass. Pull out the video camera and film your most attractive friend putting condiments up his ass for some erotic men's site. Sure it seems a little embarrassing, but there's no way anyone's ever going to see it and you'll both make £500.

"Wait, you too?" Yeah, I was in the DON'Ts a few years ago, then I got this invitation to come here for the weekend. Apparently some rich guy was in the DON'Ts too and wants us all to get together to plan revenge. "Oh shit. Like that movie *The Benchwarmers*?" Yeah. "I fucking loved that movie." Me too. Jon Lovitz is my dawg.

Her "up for a larf" demeanour, Coke Bust t-shirt and quirky green Wellingtons have rosy-cheeked hardcore boys (who only ever halfway fucked one other girl before) trailing her around the show like confused puppies.

If you're packing butter-smooth, warm-yet-slightly-moist perfect tits underneath your snappy little black dress, you might want to bring your flamingest homo friend out with you to scare away the legions of horny pigs that will be watching your every move. Don't worry. "Chevy II" there has got your back.

If you're gonna take one part of an outfit and turn it all the way up to 11, why'd you have to turn up turn-ups? Those things SUCK. Were you not satisfied with getting home and just finding grit and cigarette butts in there? You wanted to move on to bigger and grosser things?

People like this make me wonder if the al-Qaeda take requests.

Why is it that Hispanics always make the best transsexuals? Maybe cause their mums train them to put on make-up and laugh at their pee-pees in the bath.

For some reason this guy is awesome. Look at how focused he is! And what do you think is in his backpack? Bet it's full of hot dogs.

That thing on her head isn't just some goofy hat for a meth-smoking Pilates instructor to wear to a Rusted Root show. It's what Bolivian peasants use to decorate their donkeys.

Thanks for the photo, but not sure what exactly you expect us to say here. Way to die of something? Artificial resuscitation is so last season? Help us out here.

Look, they know you're not going to be giving it up for them anytime soon and they wouldn't know what to do with it if you did, but old dudes have an entire encyclopaedia of sexual data in their heads, so when you throw them a 10-second courtesy flirt you're actually giving a scientist a hundred Rubik's Cubes he can sit and mull over for the rest of the year.

You already know that sloppy Fall Out Boy whores reek like stale smoke and bubblegum and have more shit in their purse than you have in your house. But did you also know that they secretly use the piss of nanny goats to dye their hair? Bet you didn't!

FARTING Girls can never fart, no matter what. If they feel they have one coming on, they have to go the bathroom with a pack of matches. They can also never openly admit to pooing. That means running the taps when it comes out and NEVER walking into the bathroom with a magazine. Boys can fart in front of girls after six months of dating or 100 fucks (whichever comes first).

When you're the best man at a gay wedding, it is strictly forbidden to fart at the altar. After an hour-long ceremony, the trumpeting pressure built up from the afternoon's vegan canapes reaches such a peak that it makes you want to rip off your pants, wrench open the nearest window, and let rip with a long, pungent anal symphony of highs and lows so mellifluous they create a new musical scale.

This guy's great because nobody in his LARPing community has any idea how enormous his uncircumcised penis is, and once they find out the source of his dark wizardry he'll have already butt-fucked half the water pixies and chaotically aligned bards in the UK.

This guy's Hitler moustache and affinity for parakeets are both terrifying and fascinating. Something tells me he was a fringe invite to his own wedding.

Doing pull-ups on a street sign is something you can only do when you're black. Delicate faux lumberjacks with the five-o'clock shadows of Mesoamerican transsexuals should just stick to slouching.

This guy should roll a ten-sided die that, instead of numbers, bears life-choice options like "Find actual human vagina" and "Living with Mum is more conformist than you thought".

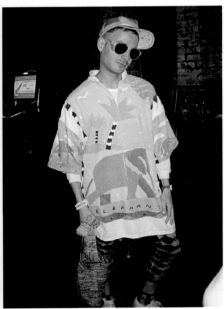

I like this sleazy Hungarian hipster's style. If he weren't so fat you'd think, "Wow, he probably gets laid a lot," 'cause he's sort of creepy and lascivious in that vampire kind of way girls often dig. But then you notice the meat puppet he's been dragging around and realise, damn, he actually gets laid a lot regardless.

Look at this little neon Beastie Boi. Did he not get the Jay-Z memo about "all-black everything"? This is exactly the type of kid who gets taken from the bus station by a creep pretending to look for his "muse".

This is the type of house that is filled with trash, smells like soup, has a black-and-white TV and everyone dresses like they won a £15 shopping spree at a secondhand shop, but then there's a wall of desks lined with brand-new MacBook Airs. I'd like to dick-punch these guys repeatedly.

Ninety percent of the time a white guy with dreads will look like an asshole 100 percent of the time, and 60 percent of the time redheads act creepy 99 percent of the time, which makes this guy a total and complete nightmare numbers-wise.

There's nothing hotter than a skate crew. It doesn't even have to be made up of cute, gawky teens. You could be a pimply Mars Volta fan, a 28-year-old frat reject or even a Chinese banker's gay son—as long as you're ripping the streets together we'll still want to bust a nut all over your shoes.

Wait... Shit.

BABIES After college, girls have to decide if they want babies or a career. If you think you're going to be a graphic designer and then stop everything at 36, find the right guy, have the baby, and then go back to your career when the kid starts pre-school, you are sadly mistaken. Your eggs are shit at 36. Don't get mad at us, it's God's fault. So if you don't want to be a lonely spinster who watches *Sex and the City* like it's on fire, get over careers and find a reliable man.

P.S. Careers aren't that great anyways; it's not all golf and strip clubs, it's mostly putting out fires and worrying about lawyers.

Hey shit-for-brains, it's called a condom.

Fuck having a family.

DOs

Never has "caught in flagrante" looked so relaxed. Ah right...he's stoned out of his fucking mind.

There's a stop on the express train to full-blown crazy where your self-confidence and self-awareness are at such perfect levels that even a snuggie, two kilos of English teacher jewellery and a purse made out of MySpace makes perfect sense.

This guy was in a band in college. They played local gigs. The guitarist quit and went to law school. They broke up. He now works at an insurance company. He compensates for the dead dream by getting uncomfortably drunk and raging way too hard in low-key situations.

This is the type of guy I have nightmares about: a college jerk-off who has never met a black person, wears "funny" boxer shorts, thinks he's the only one who understands the nonsequential humour of *Family Guy*, and is not afraid to freestyle rap in any situation at any time regardless of how much secondhand embarrassment it's causing the people around him.

Our resolution for 2011 is to cull the boring "this town sucks" whiners from our pool of friends so we can focus our full attention on the ones who turn another year with nothing to do from "Oh my" and "A boo-hoo" into "Woo-hoo" and "Give me some more K."

Whoa, dude, nice Koosh ball hat! You know what would be the perfect accessory? A dick in your mouth.

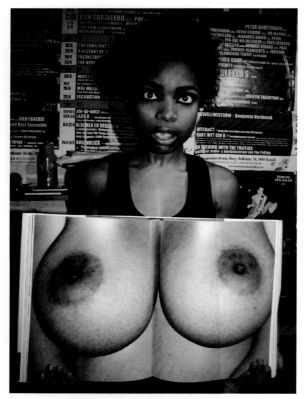

Feminists and Joe Francis have made it so the only time you can ask a girl to show you her tits without feeling like a rapist asshole is when she's carrying them around in a book.

It's kind of cool seeing places like Venezuela and Hungary get their own *Ugly Betty* franchise, but someone really needs to step up the QC.

DOs

I want to have a bite of that juicy little package while we sit in bed and read the obituaries together.

Well aren't we a scrumptious little dawber? Aren't we a dinky little doozer, dancing around the kitchen in our wee black undies? Aren't we a diddly widdle doodlebee? Aren't we a cheeky widdle monkeybug, pat-pat patacaking some little patties to put in our wum-wum? God I am hard right now.

JUST EAT SOMETHING Be aware that you are a nicer person when you aren't really hungry.

Do whatever it takes man. Lie your brain to smithereens if it means taking this fucking cock grenade home. Tell her you're the Emperor of Fucking Rome if need be.

Um, if you're trying to convince folks not to turn London into New Sodom you might want to track down a better artist, because that crummy Mike Diana rip-off is seriously making us want to fire up some Obituary and see if we can still squeeze into our old cock ring.

DOs

Seeing European tramps like Bruno S (RIP) hold their shit together and retain a touch of class always makes me wonder how often there but for the grace of a scarf and hat go our bums.

While mums think a pair of checkered Vans and mismatched socks is all it takes to retain their "kooky" cred, the real lifers are too focused on finding shoes that go with Betsey Johnson lounge troll to even care.

It's one thing to parade around in a beehive wig and stilettos looking like a character in a Broadway show about transvestites—those guys are abominable. But a man in Barnes & Noble scouting for his next great read in a pair of sensible heels? Now that's awesome.

This is a good look for a woman in her early 20s, if by "good look" you mean "destitute middle-aged Ukrainian prostitute who's been walking directly into the wind".

DOs

It's cute to force your religious beliefs on your pet, but just remember what happened to another wiseguy who tried to do that by the name of Dr Moreau. He wound up getting his balls ripped off by a pack of raging manimals, and I don't even think he was Jewish.

The next time you buy Tupperware, remember that there is a 99.9 percent chance that somebody got fucked on it.

The "tucked-in, ribbed, quarter-zip satanic goth at a wine bar" style is about as badass as a kitten puking a rainbow.

Oh cool, it's The Fear in sweating, jiggly, hairy human form. Have fun screaming and begging for mercy as he chases you down the corridors of every bad acid trip you've ever had.

ONE NIGHT ON, ONE NIGHT OFF One of the oldest roadie rules of survival is never party two nights in a row. You have to stay in and recover every second night. If your girlfriend still thinks this is too much, you may tell her to fuck off. The day after your recovery, you should be getting some kind of exercise or something because you are a fat piece of shit.

The secret to partying is to deserve it. When you go out every night the whole thing becomes a big boring chore, but when you just finished a huge project and everyone else is happy to be there the night is so fun you wish your brain recorded video.

Damp country lanes were designed by the gods as places for you to take pretty girls with better taste than you in books. If you're lucky, she'll let you dry-hump her on the grass for a while until a couple of joggers get too close and she gets sketched out.

PS: This is the kind of moment you'll be lamenting to your shrink when you're 45

I know the old-timey aesthetic of curly moustaches and straight-razor shaving is popular with 20-somethings these days, but this is just too much. You know what would tie this moron's outfit together nicely? A cane pulling him out of the frame by his neck and a bout of scarlet fever.

DOs

It started with a small part in a commercial for Tampax that turned into a role as a hot alien on an episode of *Babylon 5*. Then things got slow and that's how you end up in Vegas dancing on a display yacht at a nude boat expo to pay for your health insurance.

This is what I imagine everyone in Europe between the ages of 18 and 28 looks like on any random afternoon: slightly androgynous, zany but in a manageable way, extremely positive attitude, and on their way to hang a futuristic-looking lamp somewhere. I don't know how someone was able to take a picture inside my brain, but whatever, I'm into it.

Question: Of the guy who looks like a lesbian, the non-threatening black guy with a post-irony ironic trucker hat, and the guy in a bicycle helmet who's not on a bike, who is least likely to get invited to my birthday party?

Whether he's an Icelandic deep-house enthusiast who thinks it's still 1995 or a Fijian mash-up DJ from the year 2021 who's so on the cutting edge of every emerging trend that it's actually intimidating, this guy is the worst.

Life is beautiful for people who refuse to be jaded by it. Even in the bleak-est, most miserable of all situations there's always little glints of hope and joy peeking through the awfulness. Never stop looking for them.